Dead last finish is greater than did not finish, which trumps did not start

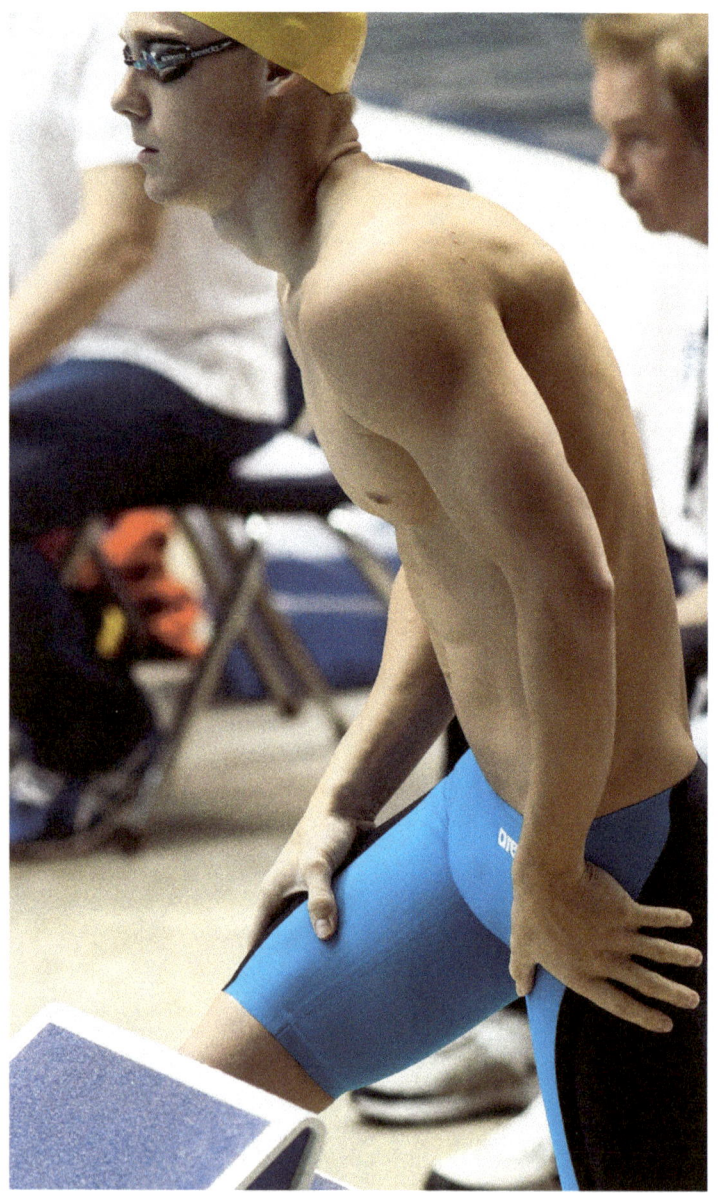

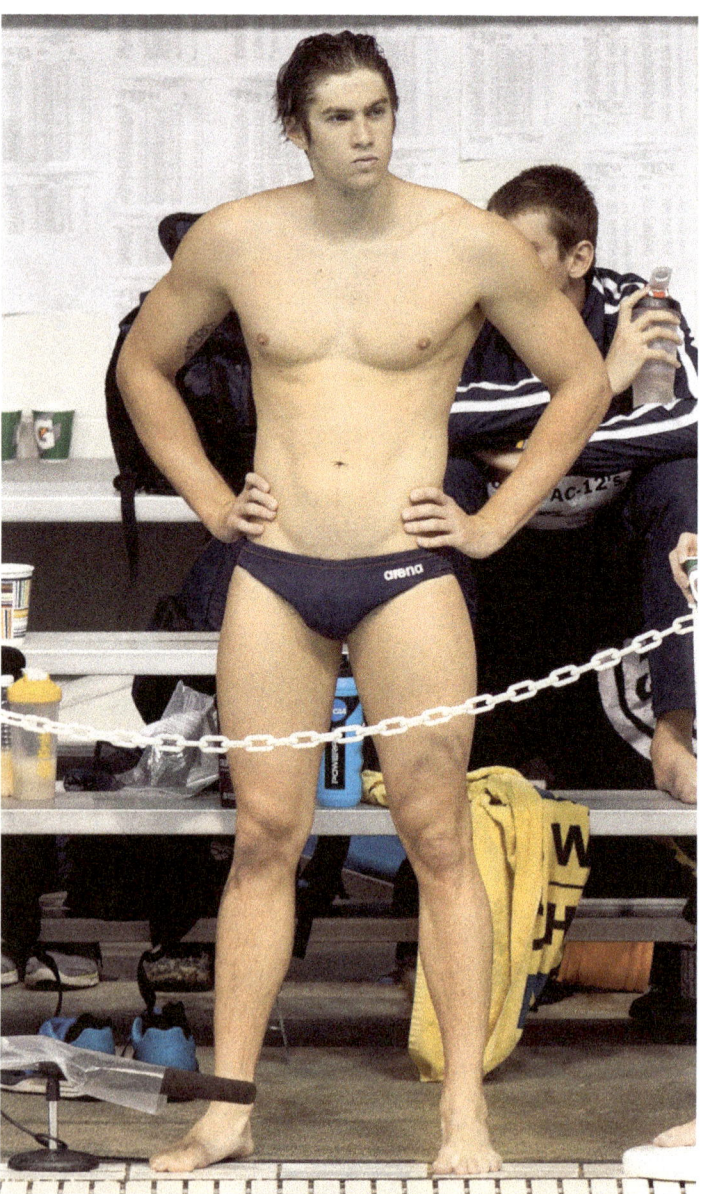

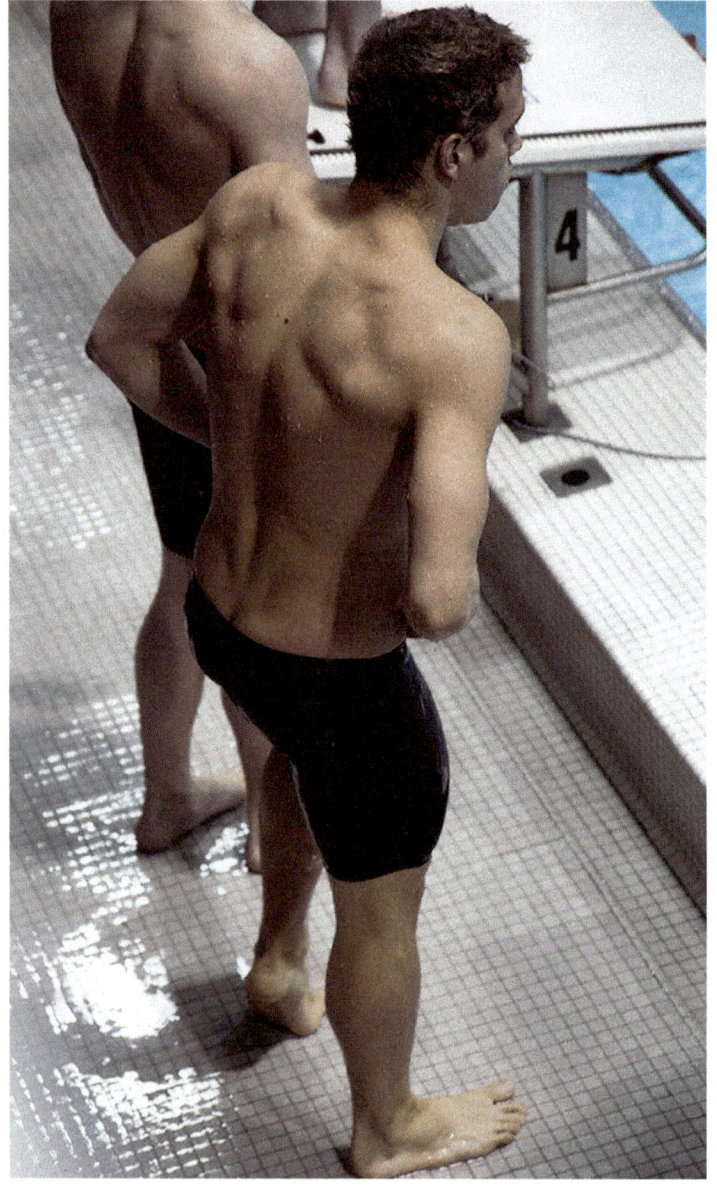

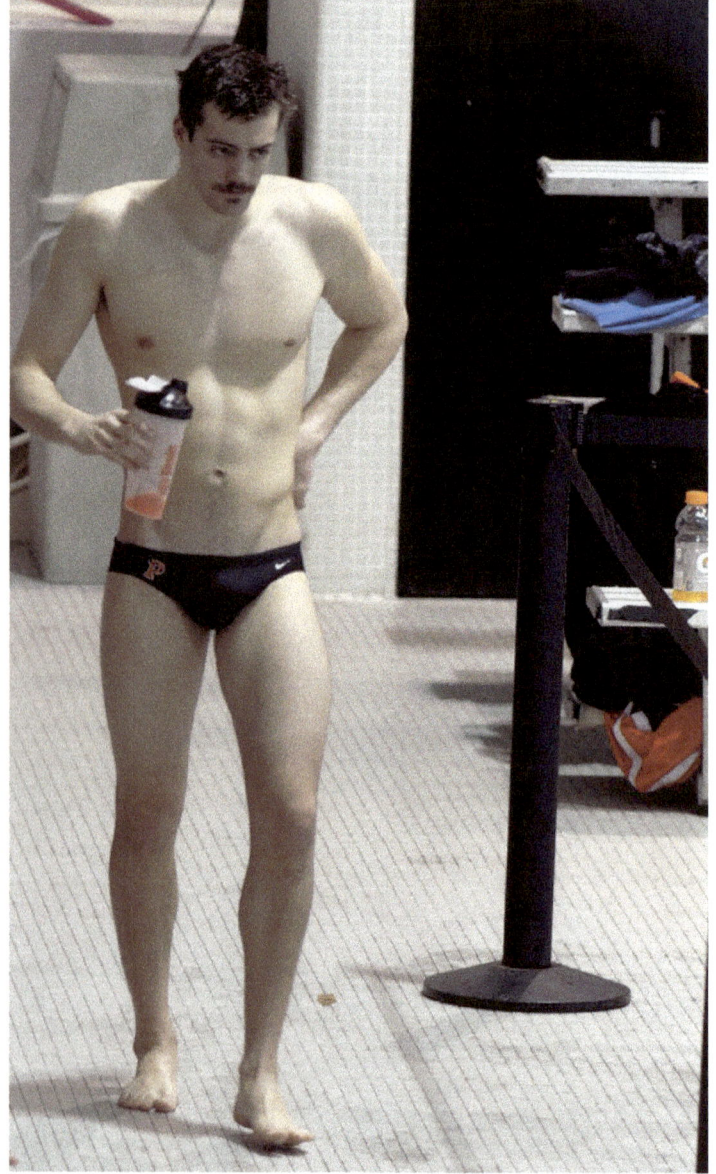

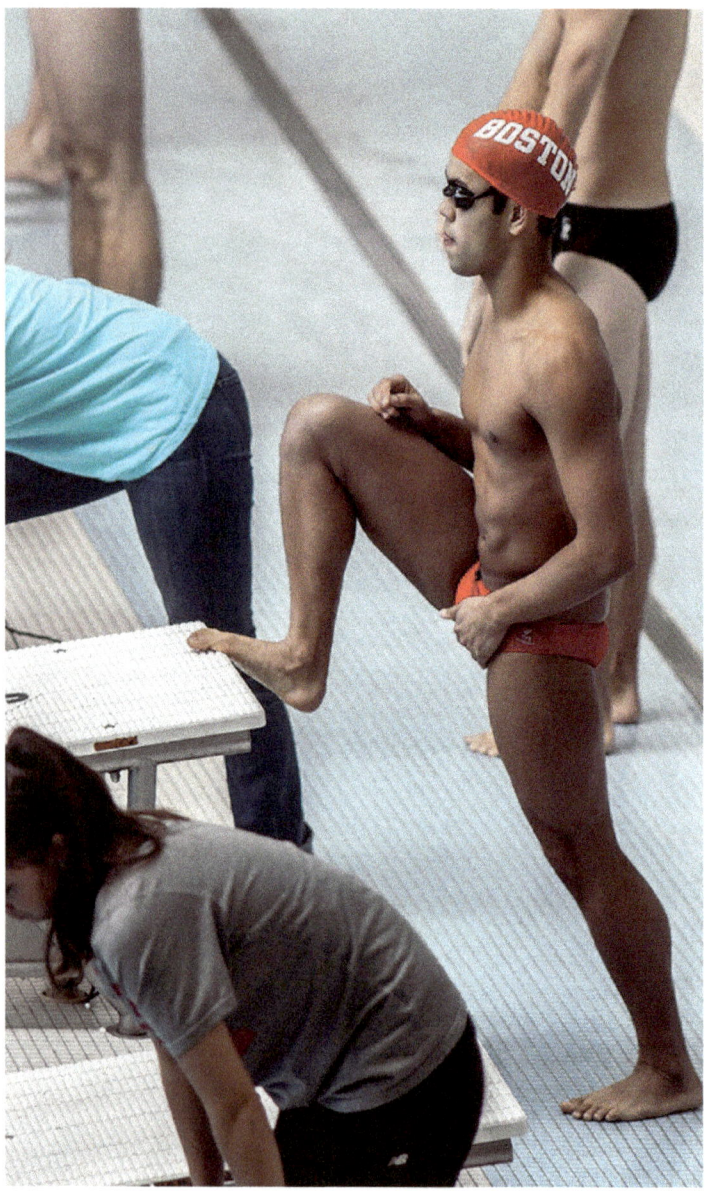

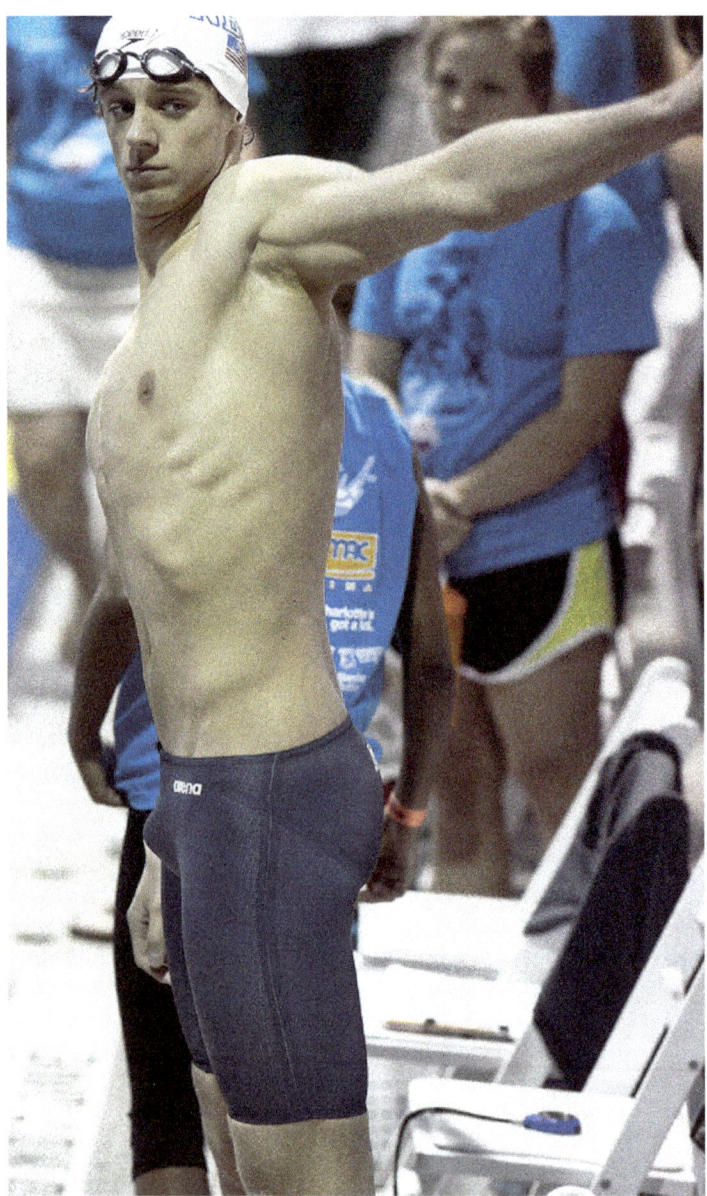

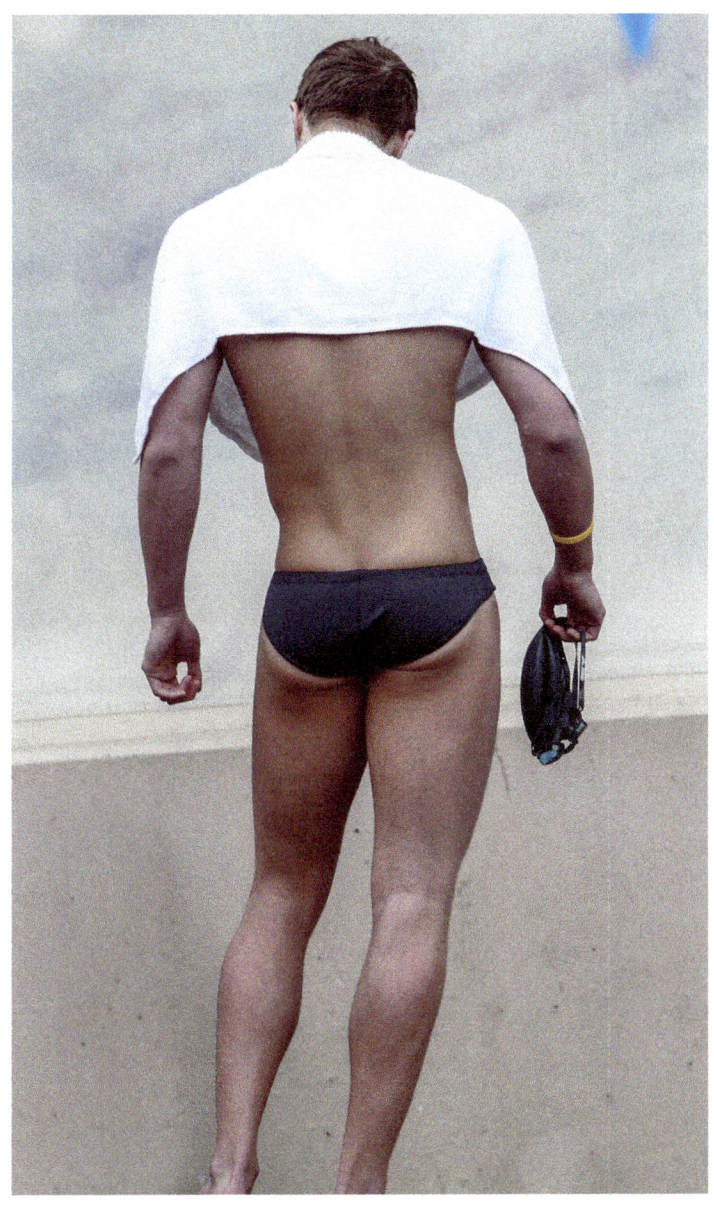

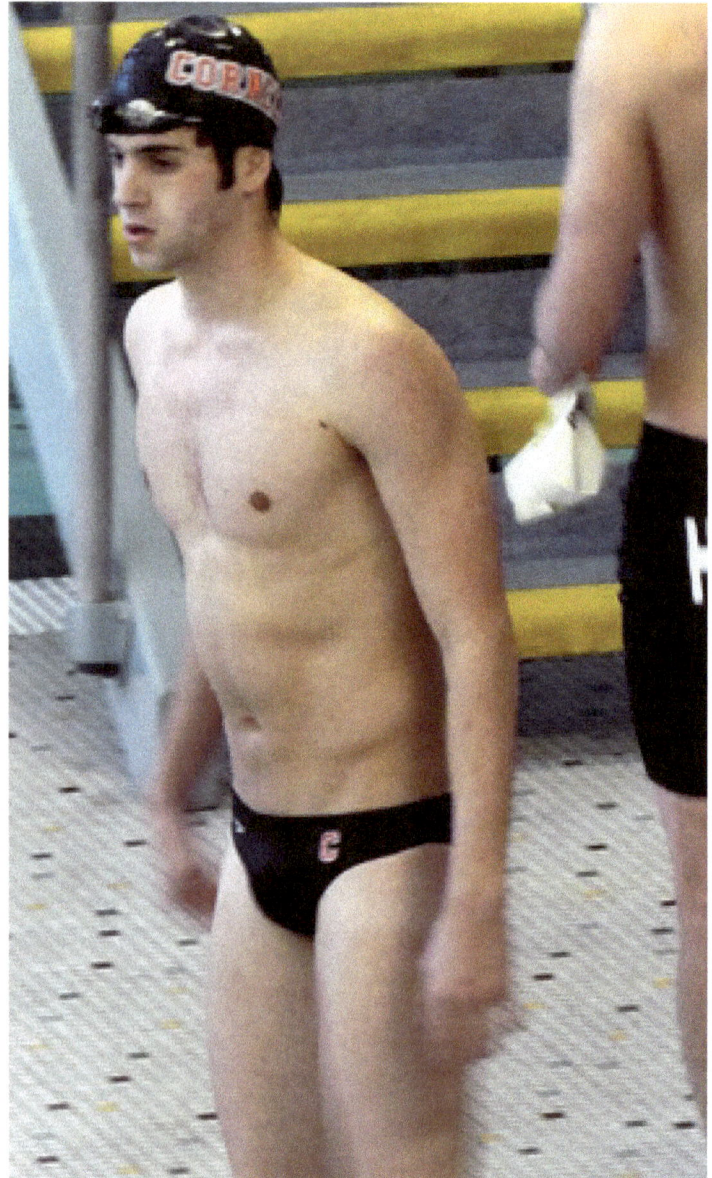

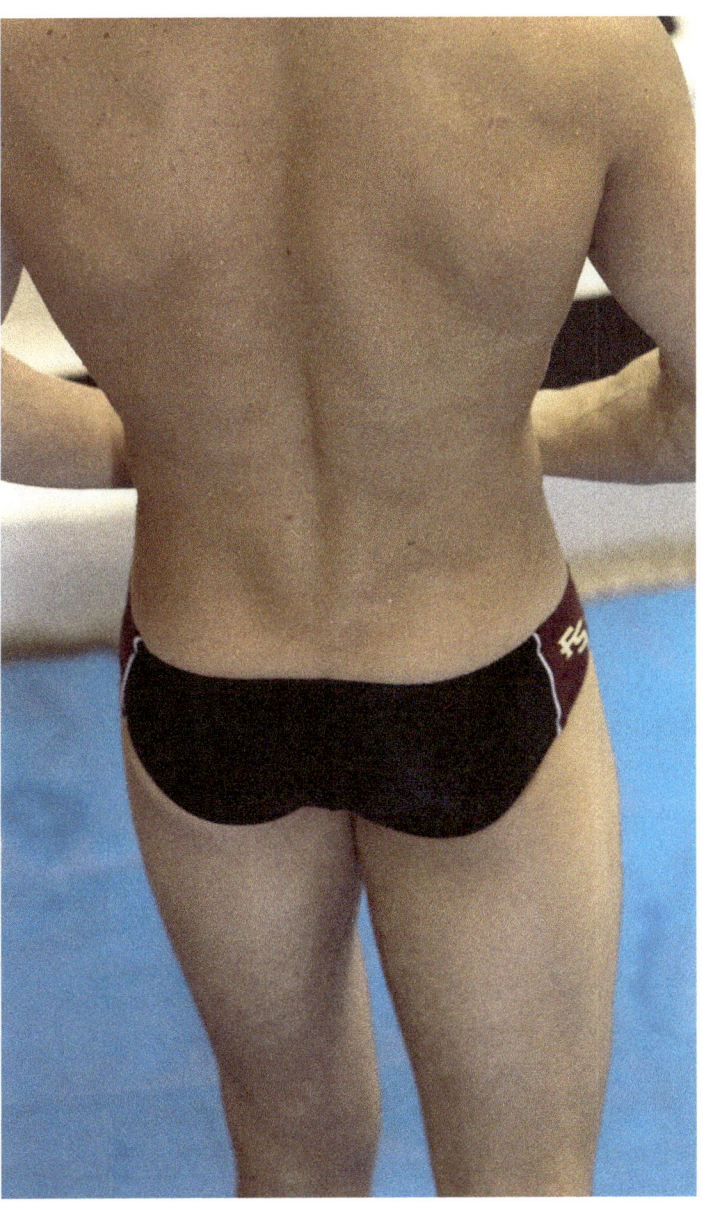

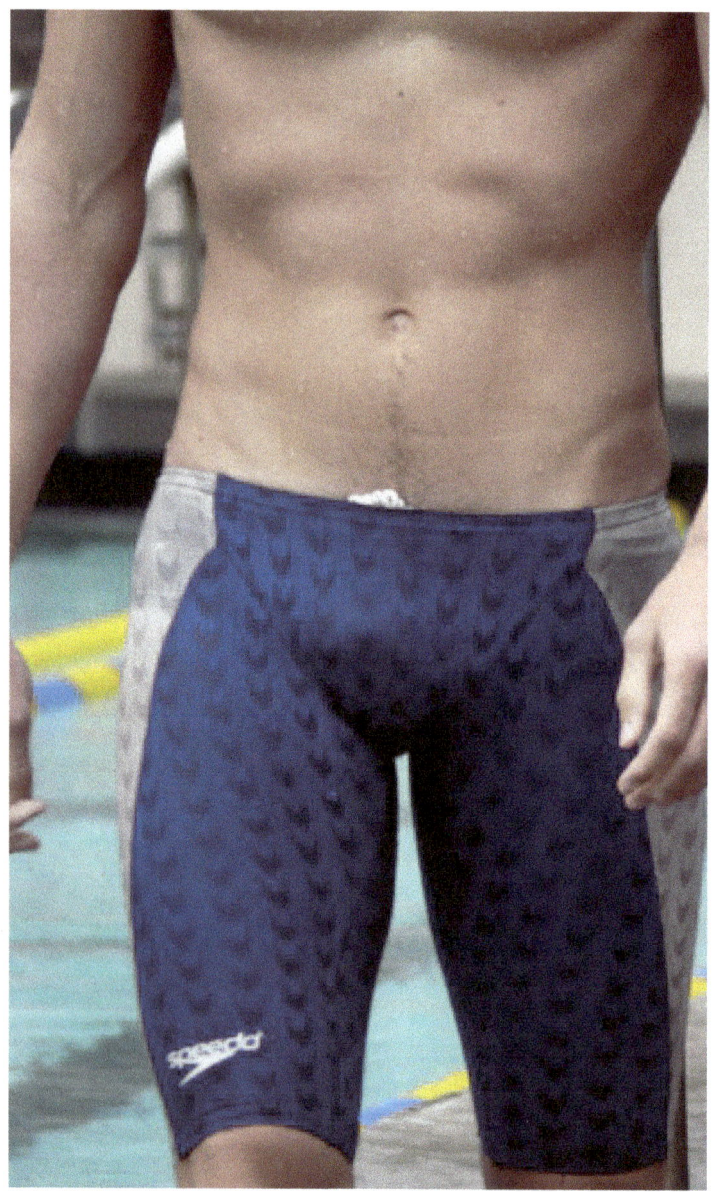

CPSIA information can be obtained
at www.ICGtesting.com
Printed in the USA
BVHW021410060619
550351BV00015B/451/P

9 780368 876462